STORY TIME ONE

STORY TIME
ONE

Pamela Dowman

**Illustrated by
Gwen Gibson**

**SCRIPTURE UNION
5 Wigmore Street, London W1H OAD**

© Scripture Union 1967
First published 1967
Reprinted in this format 1969
Reprinted 1972
Reprinted 1973
Reprinted 1974
ISBN 0 85421 165 9

Printed in Malta by St Paul's Press Ltd

Contents

Jesus and the children

Do you like going out with Mummy and Daddy? Do you sometimes go to see people together? I expect you go to Grandma's or Auntie's sometimes. It's exciting and you don't mind getting up early on days when something special is going to happen, do you?

A little boy and a little girl lived in a country far away across the sea. We do not know their names but we will call them Ben and Mary. They lived in a white house, which had a flat roof. There were stairs to their house but they

6

were outside. That's a funny place to have them, isn't it? But when they climbed up the stairs, they could go on the flat roof, and look out over all the other houses. Ben's and Mary's friends lived in houses like that too.

One morning Mummy woke up early, and she woke the children.

'Wake up, Ben! Wake up, Mary! We're going out today to see someone special. We don't want to be late.'

'Where are we going?' asked Ben.

'We're going to see Jesus, because He's staying near here,' said Mummy.

'Oh! good,' said Mary. 'Come on, Ben. We want to see Him because He's kind. He tells lovely stories.'

Ben and Mary got up quickly. They couldn't make their beds though like you can. Their beds didn't have any legs either. They had been sleeping on mat beds on the floor. So when they got up, they rolled up their mats and put them away. Then Ben and Mary helped Mummy to tidy the house.

At last they were all ready to go and see Jesus. 'Come along,' said Mummy. 'We're all ready.' It was very hot, and they didn't need to wear hats or coats. They just went out into the sunshine to go to see Jesus together.

7

How do you think they were going to get to Jesus? They might have gone in a train, mightn't they? But there were no trains. They might have gone in a bus — but there were no buses. They might have gone in a car — but there were no cars either. They were going to walk all the way.

Ben and Mary began to hop, skip and jump along the road. They were excited. They were going to see Jesus. They passed lots of little houses just like theirs, with flat roofs and stairs outside.

Ben and Mary met some of their friends as they walked along.

'We're going to see Jesus,' said Ben.

'So are we,' said their friends.

A little way along the road they met some more friends.

'We're going to see Jesus,' said Mary.

'So are we,' said their friends.

At last they came round a corner . . . and . . . yes, there was Jesus.

'Goody,' said Mary. 'There's Jesus.'

'Hooray,' said Ben, 'we've found Him,' and they both ran to Him.

But it wasn't quite how they had thought it would be. Some of Jesus' friends were there. They saw the children coming and they looked very cross. The children were a little afraid and sad.

'Go away,' said one of the friends. 'Jesus can't be bothered with you today. He's too tired.'

How disappointed they were. They had so wanted to see Jesus. Ben wanted to cry, and Mary did cry a little bit. Some of the other girls cried too, and they hid their faces in their mummies' clothes.

Then they heard a voice that was quite different. 'It's all right, children. I do want to see you. Come back.' The children turned . . . and saw . . . yes, Jesus with His arms out waiting for them.

They all ran to Jesus and hugged Him and told Him their news, and then they all sat down and He told them stories. Jesus was the best story-teller in all the world, and the children listened and listened. Then He put His hands on them and prayed for them and their baby brothers and sisters as well.

After a long time — although it didn't seem very long — they said 'goodbye,' and 'thank You' to the Lord Jesus. Then they went home together laughing and talking about all the lovely things Jesus had told them.

Jesus loved Ben and Mary and their friends. Jesus loves *all* children, everywhere. He loves *you* and your brothers and sisters, and the children who live next door to you, and all the children in the world.

A Prayer

Dear Lord Jesus, thank You for loving Ben and Mary and all their friends, Thank You for loving me and all my friends, too. Amen.

The Good Shepherd

I wonder if you have ever been lost? Perhaps you were shopping with Mummy and suddenly you couldn't find her. You could see lots of other coats and legs and shoes but you couldn't see your Mummy's coat or shoes. Perhaps you felt frightened, and when Mummy found you I expect you held her hand.

This story is about a sheep who was lost once. We don't know his name, but we will call him Woollie. He lived with lots of other sheep. There were one hundred altogether. There were some mummy sheep, some daddy sheep and some lambs. Of course, Woollie and his friends didn't look after themselves. They had a very good shepherd who looked after them and he knew each one of his sheep.

One day, Woollie went out with his shepherd and all his friends. The shepherd took them to a place where there was some green grass. They liked eating that. Then they went over some rough, stony ground and the sheep didn't like that because there was nothing to eat. Then they came to some thorn bushes. Some of Woollie's friends got their wool caught on the thorns and prickles. The shepherd helped them to get untangled.

The shepherd knew that the sheep would need a drink, so he took them to a stream and they drank the cool, fresh water.

Then Woollie found another patch of good juicy grass.

'This is good,' thought Woollie. 'I must have some more of this.' So he went on and on chewing the green grass. But Woollie didn't see that the shepherd had gone on somewhere else. His friends had gone too.

Woollie went on eating all by himself and presently he came to a place that was very hard to walk on. There were big stones and big holes in the ground. Woollie was stumbling over the stones and suddenly his foot slipped and he fell into a big hole.

Woollie looked around. There he was in a hole and he couldn't see what to do. It was too steep to climb out. He was so sad and miserable and lonely, and it was beginning to get dark. 'Baa,' said Woollie, but no one heard him.

I wonder what the shepherd was doing? I wonder if he knew he had lost Woollie?

When it began to get dark, the shepherd led his sheep into a safe place where they would sleep for the night. The shepherd stood at the doorway and counted them all. He counted, 'One, two, three, four, five, six, seven, eight, nine, ten.' He went on and on counting until he got to ninety-five, ninety-six, ninety-seven, ninety-eight, ninety-nine — but there was one missing — he should have one hundred. Oh, dear! He must go to find the lost sheep. It was Woollie. He must find him.

Off he went to look in all the places where he had taken his sheep that day. He looked in the place where they had eaten green grass. He called, but he couldn't hear his sheep. He looked and looked but he couldn't see his sheep.

He came to the thorn bushes with all the prickles. Perhaps his lost sheep was caught in the prickles. He called again, but he couldn't hear his sheep. He looked and looked but he couldn't see his sheep.

Then he went along the stream. He called again, but he couldn't hear his sheep. He looked all along the stream, but he couldn't see his sheep.

He walked on over the patch of good juicy grass. 'Where can my sheep be?' he thought. 'I must find him.'

The shepherd came to a place where it was very hard to walk. There were big stones, and big holes in the ground. Sometimes he hurt his toe on a big stone, and then his foot slipped into a hole.

Perhaps his sheep was here somewhere. He called. He heard a little noise, 'Baa.' He called again. 'Baa.' There was Woollie. How happy the shepherd was, and so was Woollie when he saw the shepherd!

The shepherd bent over the hole and carefully lifted Woollie out. Then he put him on his shoulder and carried him all the way back to his friends.

16

He was a good shepherd, wasn't he? He knew that one of his sheep was missing. He knew it was Woollie, and he went on calling and looking until he found him.

Jesus is like a shepherd of boys and girls. You're like the sheep, and Jesus looks after you just like that good shepherd looked after Woollie and his friends.

A Prayer

Dear Lord Jesus, thank You for being my Shepherd. I'm glad that I'm one of Your lambs. Please look after me, just as the shepherd looked after his sheep. Amen.

Blind Bartimaeus

Look at these pictures and say what you see.

Now look at these pictures and say what is missing.

Here is a story about a man who would not have been able to play that 'looking' game with you. He had a long name. He was called Bartimaeus, and he was blind.

He lived in a town a long way away called Jericho. It was a lovely town with beautiful trees and flowers. But Bartimaeus couldn't see how beautiful it was. He could see nothing at all. Everything was black and like night, and so he had to use his ears to help him to know what was happening.

Bartimaeus wasn't very happy either. People were sometimes nasty and unkind to him. They got cross with him when he couldn't see where he was going. They didn't bother to talk to him or listen to him when he had anything to say.

He wasn't able to do any work because he was blind, but every day some kind friends helped him and took him by the hand and led him to the side of a busy road. He sat down and held out a little bowl. As people passed by on their way to Jericho, they sometimes dropped some money into his bowl. Sometimes his bowl was nearly full and he could buy some food to eat. Other days it was nearly empty and he had to go to bed hungry.

Although he couldn't see what was happening in the street, he could hear things. He heard camels going by. 'Clomp, clomp, clomp,' went their feet. They went slowly. He heard donkeys going past. 'Clipperty-clop, clipperty-clop' went their feet. They went quite quickly. He could hear the sound of people's feet as they walked past too.

Well, now, I'll tell you about one very wonderful day that Bartimaeus had. The day started in just the same way as any other day. His friends took him to his usual place and the time went slowly by. 'It's a good day', thought Bartimaeus as he heard the coins falling into his bowl, and he knew that he would be able to have a good supper that night.

Bartimaeus noticed that there was a noise in the distance and as it gradually got louder he knew that a large crowd was coming.

'What is happening?' he asked someone who was passing by. 'Jesus is here,' they said. Bartimaeus had heard of Him. He knew what Jesus could do. He could make people who were ill better. He knew that Jesus could make him see, if only he could get to Him. How excited Bartimaeus was!

He cried out, 'Jesus, please help me!' The people tried to stop him. 'Be quiet,' they said. 'We want to listen to Jesus. He is telling us about God.'

What would you feel like if you were blind and you had a chance to be made better? You wouldn't be quiet, would you? He gave another cry, 'Jesus, please help me.'

Just then a wonderful thing happened. The noise of all the people stopped, and Bartimaeus heard Jesus' voice. Jesus was saying, 'Bring that man to Me.'

The people helped Bartimaeus to Jesus. Then he heard Jesus' voice speaking to him.

Jesus said, 'What do you want Me to do for
you?' Bartimaeus answered at once. 'Lord
Jesus, I want to be able to see.' Immediately
Bartimaeus could see again.
22

He could see the camels and donkeys going along the road and all the people around him. But best of all, he could see Jesus.

Do you remember how unhappy he was because people were not always kind to him, and they didn't listen when he wanted to say something?

But now he had Jesus for a Friend. He is the best Friend anyone could have because He cared about Bartimaeus and He heard when he called to Jesus. Jesus is the best Friend for you to have, too, because He loves you and cares about you. You can talk to Him about everything.

A Prayer

Dear Lord Jesus, thank You for being a Friend to Bartimaeus, and for listening when he called. Thank You for being my Friend, too. Amen.

Zacchaeus

Are you sometimes too small to see things? Do you say to Mummy or Daddy, 'Please lift me up to see'? I expect Daddy puts you on his
24

shoulder and then you can see everything. A little man in this story did some climbing, because he wanted to see Jesus.

He was only a *little* man, but he had a *long* name. It was Zacchaeus. He was only a *little* man, but he was very greedy and selfish. He wanted everything for himself and he wouldn't share things with other people. He just kept on thinking of all the things Zacchaeus would like. His job was to collect money for the king, but he always took too much. One day, he collected money from a man whom we'll call Mr. Simeon. He made Mr. Simeon give him two silver coins, and when he got home he put one silver coin in the box for the king and kept one silver coin for himself. So, you see, he really was greedy.

Zacchaeus had lots of money and a beautiful home with lovely things inside and he could buy anything he wanted. But he wasn't very happy, even with all those things he had. He was very lonely because he had no friends.

One day Zacchaeus looked out of his house and saw crowds of people hurrying down the road. 'Oh!' said Zacchaeus. 'Something exciting must be happening. I'll see what it is.'

He hurried out of his house and down the road to where there was a big crowd of people.

'What's going on here?' he asked. 'What are you all waiting for?'

Someone told him that Jesus was coming. Jesus was a wonderful man. He loved to help ill people and sad people and bad people.

'I want to see Jesus,' said Zacchaeus, but he couldn't see anything just then because he was at the back of the crowd. He was such a little man that he couldn't see over the heads of the people. You know what that's like, don't you? The people pushed in front of him and elbowed him out of the way. They wouldn't let

Zacchaeus get in front. They didn't like Zacchaeus and they weren't going to make a place for him.

Now when Zacchaeus wanted something very much he always thought of a way to get it. And he wanted to see Jesus.

'Ha! Ha!' he thought. 'There's a big sycamore tree a bit farther down the road. Jesus will come past that way, so I'll climb up and sit in the tree, and I'll be able to see everything.'

He ran on down the road, climbed up into the tree and waited. Presently, Jesus and His friends came along. They were walking quite slowly because there were such a lot of people all trying to see Jesus. Now Zacchaeus could see them, and he peeped out of the tree to have a good look. Suddenly, Jesus stood still. 'What's the matter?' thought Zacchaeus. 'Perhaps He's stopping to make somebody better again.' But then he heard his own name. 'Zacchaeus,' and Jesus was looking up into the tree and calling to him. 'Zacchaeus, hurry out of that tree. I'm coming to your house today.' 'Jesus is calling me,' thought Zacchaeus. 'Jesus is coming to *my* house.' He was so surprised that he nearly *fell* out of the tree, but he climbed down as quickly as he could. 'Come along, Jesus,' he said, 'I'll show You where my house is.'

Zacchaeus was very happy, but the other people weren't happy. They grumbled and said, 'Why has Jesus gone to stay with Zacchaeus? He is a nasty, bad man.'

The people went on grumbling and they stayed outside Zacchaeus' house to see what would happen.

Suddenly, Zacchaeus stood up and said, 'Lord Jesus, I want to be different now I've met You, because You are my Friend. I've been very greedy and selfish and I don't want to be any more. I'll go and give my money to the poor people instead. And I must go and give some money back to Mr. Simeon. I took two silver coins from him, and I kept one for myself. I'll give him four silver coins back now for himself.' So when Zacchaeus met Jesus, he became quite different, didn't he?

A Prayer

Lord Jesus, help me to be like Zacchaeus when You were his Friend. Help me to be sorry when I do naughty things, and to put them right. Amen.

Four kind friends

Once there was a man who was very ill. He was so ill that he couldn't move himself at all. All day and all night he had to lie flat on a mattress. It was very sad because there were so many things that he couldn't do.

He couldn't walk along the road to the shops. He couldn't jump over a puddle. He couldn't climb over a gate. He couldn't turn head-over-heels. He couldn't throw and catch a ball. He could only lie flat on his mattress.

Sometimes his friends came to visit him. Sometimes they came to tell him about what they had been doing. One day one of his friends came to see him, and he said:

'Do you know what happened yesterday? That man called Jesus was on the shore of the lake and there were crowds of people all around listening to Him. It was very difficult for everyone to hear what He was saying. You'll never guess what He thought of doing! He borrowed a rowing boat, and then let the boat float at the edge of the water so that He could stand up and talk to everyone on the sea-shore.

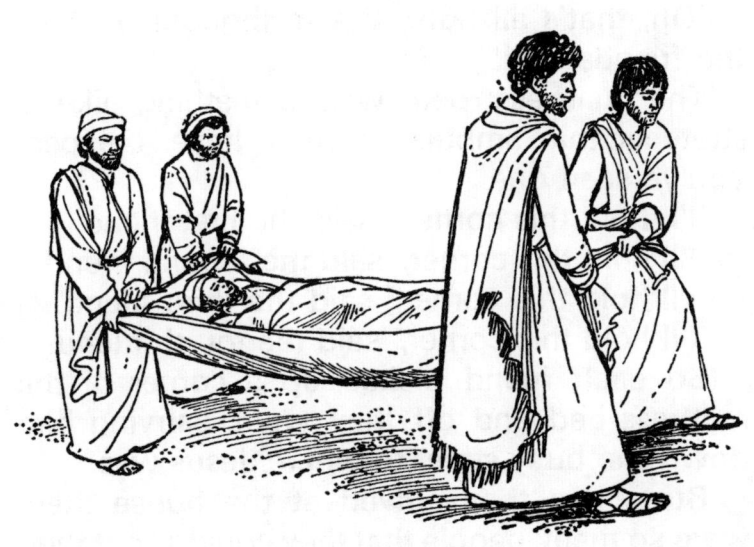

He's a wonderful man. He told us some stories to help us to understand about God, and what God wants us to do.'

The sick man liked to hear all the news from his friends. He wished that he could be outside seeing everything that was happening.

One day, when he was lying quietly on his mattress, four of his friends came into the house. They were terribly excited.

'Jesus is coming here,' said one. 'We're going to take you to see Him, so that He can make you better,' said another of his friends.

'But how could I get there?' asked the man.

'Oh, that's all right. We've thought of that,' the friends said.

The mattress bed was something like a stretcher that ambulance men have. I expect you've seen one.

'I'll hold this corner,' said the first friend.

'I'll hold this corner,' said the second friend.

'I'll hold this corner,' said the third friend.

'I'll hold this corner,' said the fourth friend.

So each friend picked up a corner of the mattress bed and off they went, carrying him down the busy street to where Jesus was.

But when they arrived at the house there were so many people that they couldn't get their friend on the mattress anywhere near to Jesus.

32

They knew that Jesus loved sick people and that He would love their sick friend, so they had to find a way of getting him there.

The friends looked at the house. It was one of those white houses with a flat roof and steps outside going up to the roof. It gave them an idea. They began to carry their sick friend on his mattress bed up the stairs and on to the roof.

Then they began to pull away some of the roof and soon they had a big hole. They put some ropes on to the corners of the mattress bed and slowly passed their sick friend down through the big hole to Jesus underneath.

When Jesus saw the friend who was ill, He loved him very much. Because He loved him He wanted to make him well again. But Jesus also knew that this man had done lots of naughty things too. So first of all Jesus looked at the man who was ill and said, 'I forgive you all the naughty things you have ever done. I won't remember them any more

Then Jesus said, 'Get up, roll up your mattress and walk home.'

And that poor man who couldn't use his arms, or legs, got up and walked out of the house. His friends didn't have to carry him this time. He was well again! He could walk as well

as his friends. He could run. He could jump. He could clap his hands. Because Jesus loved him He had made him well again.

A Prayer

Dear Lord Jesus, help me to think of kind things I can do for all the people I know. Amen.

The nobleman's son

What would your Mummy do if, one morning when you woke up, you felt so ill you had to stay in bed? Yes, she would send for the doctor. She might talk to him on the telephone and tell him what was wrong with you, but could he make you better while he stayed at his own house? No, he would have to come along and see you.

Once, there was a boy who was very, very ill. We don't know what his name was but we'll call him Peter. Peter lived in a lovely house because his daddy worked for the king and was rich.

Each day when Peter's daddy came home he would run to meet him and tell him all about what he had been doing.

One day when his daddy came home there was no Peter running to meet him as usual.

'I wonder where Peter is?' he asked himself.

When Daddy got indoors Mummy told him. 'Peter's in bed,' she said. 'He's very ill. He hasn't been out to play all day.'

Daddy went to see Peter. He was lying on

his little mattress bed on the floor; his head hurt all over. He didn't want any lunch or tea.

Peter's daddy was very sad. He had lots of money, but there was nothing he could buy to make Peter better. He asked some doctors to make Peter better, but no one knew what to do.

One day, Peter's daddy said, 'I know what

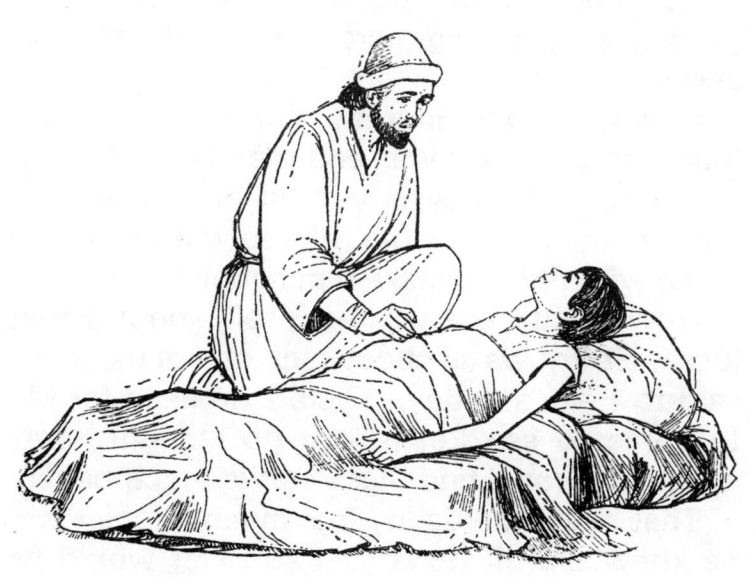

I'll do. I'll go and tell Jesus. He will help me.'

Wasn't that a good thing for him to do? Of course Jesus will always listen when we talk to Him. So off he went, as fast as he could go, to find Jesus.

He couldn't go by car because there were no cars.

He couldn't go by bus because there were no buses.

He couldn't go by train because there were no trains.

He couldn't go by bicycle because there were no bicycles.

He rode on his horse instead. He went galloping, galloping across the hills to find Jesus.

It was a long journey but Peter's daddy found where Jesus was and then he said, 'Lord Jesus, my little boy is very ill indeed and no one can make him better. Please will You come home with me and make him better?'

Now Jesus knew already all about Peter, just as He knows all about each one of us, so He said to Peter's daddy, 'There's no need for Me to come to see Peter. You go straight home again, and you'll find that Peter is much better.'

That made the daddy feel much happier and he knew that if *Jesus* said so Peter would be

all right, even though He hadn't *seen* Peter at all.

So he climbed on to his horse and off he went back home again.

When he was nearly home he could see people running towards him. They were some of the servants who worked in his house. When he met them one servant said, 'Master, we've got news for you!'

Another servant said, 'Your little boy is much better. He's going to be all right after all.'

The daddy said, 'That's wonderful news. When did he start to get better?'

'Yesterday, at one o'clock in the afternoon suddenly he was quite better.'

'That's just the time when Jesus told me he would be better,' the daddy said.

So now the servants understood why the little boy was better, and they all hurried home to see Peter.

Peter never *saw* Jesus but he was quite better. Jesus made him better because his daddy asked Him.

You can't see Jesus, but you can ask Him about things, and He will help you just as He helped Peter.

A Prayer

Lord Jesus, I know that You love me and are my Friend, even though I cannot see You. You helped Peter when he couldn't see You. Please look after everyone I love. Amen.

Nine who forgot

Once there were ten men. You can count them.
One, two, three, four, five, six, seven, eight,
nine, ten. We don't know their names but they
could have been names like Alphaeus, Ezekiel,
Malchus, Simeon—you haven't any friends
with those names, have you? Those ten men
were very sad and lonely because they were all
very ill. They didn't have to stay in bed all day,
but they had to keep away from everybody
else. You see, they had spots all over them, and
someone else could get the spots, too. It was
42

rather like when someone has measles or chicken-pox and they can't come out to play because someone else might catch it, too.

One man said, 'I don't think we shall ever be better.'

The second man said, 'The doctors don't know how to make us better.

All the other people who lived near said, 'You can't stay here in the town. We don't want to get all those spots. You must go away and live by yourselves. And if ever you meet anyone else, you must ring your bells, and say, "Keep away! Keep away!"

The third man said, 'What shall we have for food?'

'We will leave some food for you,' said the people. 'But you must only fetch it when we are not there. We don't want to get all those spots.'

So off went the ten men. One, two, three, four, five, six, seven, eight, nine, ten. They went out of the town, and away from all their families and friends. All the people said, 'Goodbye, and keep away from everybody. You mustn't come back here.'

Whenever they saw someone coming along the road they rang their bells, 'Ting-a-ling-a-ling.' How sad and miserable they all were.

The fourth man said, 'I wish I could see my little boy. I expect he's big enough to walk now.'

The fifth man said, 'I wish I could be with my little girl. She's big enough to help her mother with the cooking.'

The sixth man grumbled, 'We'll never get better. It's no good wishing you were at home.'

One very special day they could see several people coming along the road. They rang their bells. 'Ting-a-ling-a-ling.' They called out,

'Keep away! Keep away!' But one man kept on coming nearer and nearer to them.

They rang their bells again, 'Ting-a-ling-a-ling.' 'Keep away! Keep away!' they shouted but He took no notice. As He came nearer they could see that it was Jesus.

The seventh man said, 'It's Jesus.'

The eighth man said, 'He can do wonderful things.'

The ninth man said, 'He wants to be everyone's Friend.

The tenth man said, 'Let's ask Him to help us.'

So they called out together, 'Jesus, Master, please help us!'

Jesus stopped. He was glad they wanted Him to help them. He didn't run away from them like other people did. He looked at them all, and when they looked at Him, He looked so kind and strong. They knew He loved them. Then Jesus made them well.

Jesus said, 'Go to the man at the church and show him that you are better; then you can go home to see your families.'

So they all ran off to show that they were better. One, two, three, four five, six, seven, eight, nine, ten. All ten of them.

The first man said, 'My spots have gone.'

The second man said, 'So have mine.'

The third man said, 'We'll be able to go and see our friends.'

Just then, one man stopped. He turned round. Then he ran all the way back, until he found Jesus again.

He knelt down in front of Jesus and said,

46

'Thank You, Jesus, for making me well again.'

Then Jesus looked around, and He said, 'I thought there were ten men who had been made well. Where are the *other* nine?'

But Jesus was glad that *one* remembered to say 'Thank You.'

A Prayer

Lord Jesus, thank You for . . . . . .
(Think of all the things you want to thank Jesus for. Perhaps you will say, Mummy, Daddy, good food, toys, and fun with my friends.)

47

The picnic boy

Have you ever had a picnic? I expect Mummy has put some food in a basket, and some orange in a bottle, and off you went. Perhaps you had a picnic by the seaside or in a park or a forest.

This story is about a boy who went on a picnic with Jesus. We don't know his name, but we'll call him Mark. Mark lived with his mother and father on the shore of a lake. His father was a fisherman. He caught fish in the lake for people to eat. His mother baked bread in the oven for their breakfasts and suppers. She made the bread into shapes just like little flat, round rolls.

One day, while Mark was playing, he saw lots of people all going the same way. There were mothers and fathers, boys and girls, and some of the mothers were carrying babies.

'Where are they all going?' Mark wondered, so he asked one of the boys.

'We're going to see Jesus,' said the boy. 'He's gone over to that hill, and we're going to find Him. He tells us wonderful stories.' And he ran off.

Mark ran back to his house. 'There are lots of people going over the hill to see Jesus,' he said to his mother. 'Can I go with them?'

His mother said ,'Yes, if you like, but I'll give you a picnic to take with you, because you may get hungry.'

So Mummy found a little basket, and put in some rolls which she had baked that morning. Then she put in two little fishes which Mark's father had caught.

'Goodbye,' Mark said, and off he ran to follow the other people. He ran and ran until he caught up with them all. Then he walked along beside them. He felt rather hungry and peeped in his basket. But he wouldn't eat it now. He'd keep it for later.

At last they came to a place where crowds of people were sitting on the grass listening to a man talking to them. 'That man must be Jesus,' thought Mark. And it *was* Jesus.

Mark wanted to hear what Jesus was saying. So he crept nearer, until he was right in front of Jesus, and then he listened and listened while Jesus told a very interesting story.

When the story finished, Mark began to feel quite hungry. He thought, 'Oh, I am hungry. I'll have my picnic now.' Some of Jesus' friends thought it was getting late, and Mark heard them saying to Jesus, 'Do you think that these people should go home? They must be very hungry. They'll need something to eat.'

Mark heard Jesus say to his friends, 'You give them something to eat.'

'But how can we?' they said. 'There are so many people. We would need such a lot of money to buy bread for everyone!'

'They could have some of mine,' thought Mark. So he got up and went to one of Jesus' friends.

'Jesus could have this,' said Mark, and he gave the man his rolls and fishes.

'This boy here has five rolls and two little fishes,' said the man, 'and he wants You to have them, but they won't feed all these people, will they?'

Jesus smiled at Mark, and then He said to His friends, 'Make everyone sit down. Ask them to sit in rows.' So his friends made everyone sit down, while Mark waited with Jesus.

Jesus picked up Mark's picnic and held it in

51

His hands. 'I wonder what He's going to do with it,' thought Mark. But he didn't mind. He looked at Jesus' face, and he knew that Jesus wouldn't spoil his picnic. Jesus looked up, and

Mark heard Jesus say, 'Thank You, God our Father, for this good food. Amen.'

Then Jesus began to share out Mark's picnic, and a wonderful thing was happening. There was enough for everybody. Jesus kept giving it to His friends to give to the people. It *was* Mark's picnic. Now it was *everybody's* picnic.

Mark and all the people ate and ate until they couldn't eat any more. And Mark was so happy that he had given his picnic to Jesus.

A Prayer

Lord Jesus, please help me to share with others. Help me to share my toys and not to keep them just for myself. Amen.

Following the leader

Two men, Andrew and John, were talking one day with a friend, and they saw someone walking past. Their friend said, 'Do you see that man over there? That's Jesus. He's the One God has sent to the world'.

'Let's follow Him, and find out more about Him,' they said.

So Andrew and John followed Him. They had gone only a little way when Jesus turned round and spoke to them. He said, 'What are you looking for?' Andrew and John said, 'We'd like to know where You live.' Jesus said, 'Come and see.' They did go with Him, and they stayed for the whole day. When it was time to go home they didn't really want to leave Him ever.

But they said, 'Goodbye' and went to their own houses.

Andrew went straight home, and as he hurried along he was thinking, 'I *must* tell my brother Simon about Jesus. I'm so glad we saw Him this morning. I want to see Him often. I *must* tell Simon all about Him.' When he got home he said to Simon, 'We've had a lovely day. This morning we saw Jesus; then we followed Him. He's the One God has sent to the world. We've been with Him all day! I'm going to talk to Him often. You must meet Him, too.'

John went straight home, too. He was thinking, 'I *must* tell my brother James about Jesus. I'm so glad we saw Him this morning. I want to see Him often. I *must* tell James all

55

about Him.' When he got home he said to James. 'We've had a lovely day. This morning we saw Jesus; then we followed Him. He's the One God has sent to the world. We've been with Him all day! I'm going to talk to Him often. You must meet Him too!' So Andrew and John hadn't kept their new friend a secret.

Andrew, Simon, James and John were fishermen, and one day they were out in their fishing boats. Andrew and Simon went in their boat and James and John went in theirs. They threw their nets out and pulled them in to see if they had caught any fish. It was very hard work, but when they had caught enough fish, they pulled the boats up on the shore and began to mend the torn parts of their nets. Just then Jesus came along.

'Why, it's Jesus!' said Simon. 'We're glad to see You!'

'Good morning,' said Jesus. 'Did you catch many fish last night?'

'Oh yes, thank You, Jesus,' said Andrew.

Then Jesus said, 'Andrew and Simon, I've got a more important job for you to do than catching fish. I want you to be My helpers. I want to teach you about God, and then I want you to help Me tell other people. Will you be My friends and *follow* Me and bring other

people to Me?'

And *straightaway* Andrew and Simon said, 'Yes, we'll follow You and be Your helpers.' They wanted to go with Jesus, so now He had two helpers.

Then Jesus walked along the beach with Andrew and Simon, and there were James and John sitting in their boat, mending their nets. They had been working hard too, and their nets had some torn parts.

'Why, it's Jesus!' said John. 'We're glad to see You!'

'Good morning,' said Jesus. 'Did you catch many fish last night?'

'Oh yes, thank You, Jesus,' said James.

Then Jesus said, 'James and John, I've got a more important job for you to do than catching fish. I want you to be My helpers. I want to teach you many things about God. I want you to help Me tell other people. Will you be My friends and *follow* Me, and bring other people to Me?'

And *straightaway* James and John said, 'Yes, we'll follow You and be Your helpers.' They wanted to go with Jesus.

Now Jesus had four helpers, Simon, Andrew, James and John. They all left their fishing and they were going to do what Jesus wanted them to do They were going to learn all they could about Jesus. He was their Leader and they would follow Him. Then they could tell other people about Him.

A Prayer

Lord Jesus, I want to be one of Your helpers, like Simon, Andrew, James and John. Help me to learn, so that I can tell others about You. Amen.

Jairus' daughter

Mr. and Mrs. Jairus were very sad. Their little girl was ill. We'll call her Mary (although we're not sure of her name), and she was twelve years old. Mr. and Mrs. Jairus loved her very much and she was the only little girl they had. They were so worried and thought that she would die. No doctors could make her better.

One day Mr. Jairus said, 'I've heard that Jesus can make people who are ill better again.' Mrs. Jairus said, 'Then go and fetch Him quickly. Perhaps He will make Mary better.' So off went Mr. Jairus as fast as he could go.

When he found Jesus he knelt down in front of Him and said, 'My little girl is very ill. I think she might even die. Please come and see her, and put Your hand on her so that she will be made well.' He was delighted when Jesus started to walk along with him straightaway. 'How splendid,' thought Mr. Jairus. 'Everything's going to be all right.'

But Mr. Jairus hadn't noticed that there

were crowds of people. There were tall men and short men, fat men and thin men, tall ladies and short ladies, fat ladies and thin ladies. Everyone seemed to be there, trying to see Jesus. Some people wanted to hear what

He had to say. Other people were just a bit 'nosey' and they wanted to see if He would do anything very clever.

Mr. Jairus hurried on, showing Jesus the way to get to his house, but people did get in the way. It was very difficult to go quickly, and Mr. Jairus must get Jesus home as soon as he could He turned round to speak to Jesus, 'Come on—there's a short cut through here.' But then he saw that Jesus wasn't there. He must have gone too fast for Jesus, and He had got lost amongst all the people.

Mr. Jairus went back to find Jesus. He had to push through all those people again. At last he could see Jesus talking to a lady. She had been ill for twelve years and had spent lots of money on trying to get better. 'Fancy bothering Jesus now,' thought Mr. Jairus. 'And why doesn't He tell her to wait? He must know we have to hurry to Mary.'

But it seemed that the lady was already better. Jesus was saying to her, 'You are better because you really believed I could do it.' Mr. Jairus thought, 'Yes, and I believed He could make Mary better too. Why doesn't He hurry up?'

Just then Mr. Jairus saw one of the servants who worked at his house, and he came and said, 'Don't bother any more. Mary has died. It's too late to do anything now.' Mr. Jairus stood looking. He wanted to shout, 'It's not fair—I asked first. If *only* there hadn't been such a crowd. If *only* that lady hadn't stopped Jesus.'

Then he saw that Jesus knew what he was thinking and he was sorry that he had been cross. But he still had an ache in his throat and he wanted to get home quickly. He kept saying to himself, 'Don't be afraid, trust Jesus. Don't be afraid, trust Jesus.'

And so at last they came to his house. Everyone there was feeling sad. People were crying and making sad noises and some had flutes, on which they played sad music. Jesus said, 'Why are you making such a noise? The little girl isn't dead. She's only asleep.' That made some of the people laugh, but Jesus sent them away.

Mrs. Jairus was there and she stood very close to Mr. Jairus. 'Don't be afraid,' he said. 'Trust Jesus to make Mary better.'

Jesus went into the house with them and they stood round Mary's bed. Very gently Jesus held her hand. He said, 'Little girl, it's time to get up.' Then a wonderful thing happened. Mary opened her eyes, sat up, got

off her bed and walked. 'She must be hungry after that long sleep,' said Jesus. 'Give her something to eat.' So I expect Mrs. Jairus gave her her favourite dinner.

And Mr. Jairus thought to himself, 'So I needn't have worried after all. Jesus knew all about Mary. Jesus knows what is best.'

A Prayer

Dear Lord Jesus, I'm very glad that You know all about me and what is best for me, and for my mummy and daddy. Please look after us all. Amen.

The good Samaritan

Have you ever fallen over and hurt yourself? I expect you have, and then someone has come along to help you. Perhaps your brother or sister was kind and came and picked you up, or perhaps Mummy picked you up and washed your leg and put a plaster on it. They helped you because they loved you.

Here is a story Jesus told about a man who needed someone to be kind. Jesus didn't give him a name, but we'll call him Mr. Joab.

One day, Mr. Joab began a long walk from one town, called Jerusalem, to another town called Jericho.

'I wish I had someone to walk with me,' thought Mr. Joab. 'I hope I don't meet any bad men.'

He began his long walk. He went down the long, twisty road.

He was just going round a corner, when some bad men jumped out on him. They hit him and knocked him over.

One man said, 'I'll have his clothes.' Another man said, 'I'll take his bag. It might have some
66

money in it!' Then they jumped up among the rocks again and disappeared.

Poor Mr. Joab was hurt. He couldn't get up. His head hurt and he had some scratches on his arms and legs.

'If only someone would come and help me,' he thought.

Presently he heard footsteps coming down the road. Trit-trot, trit-trot, trit-trot. This was a man who said he loved God.

'Here's someone,' thought Mr. Joab. 'He'll help me.' But when the man saw Mr. Joab he was frightened. 'I must hurry on,' he thought. 'Some bad men might catch me too.' So he just left Mr. Joab lying in the road. He wasn't kind.

Mr. Joab felt very ill.

'I wish I could have a drink of water,' he thought. Then he could hear more footsteps. Trit-trot, trit-trot, trit-trot. Another man was coming down the road. This was a man who often went to church. 'I'm sure this man will help me,' Mr. Joab thought.

The man saw Mr. Joab lying in the road and he came to look at him. He saw that he was hurt and that he needed someone to be kind to him, but he thought, 'I must hurry on, or the bad men will catch me too.' So he left Mr. Joab lying in the road. He wasn't kind.

Mr. Joab was so unhappy. He was too hot, and he wanted a drink, and his arms and legs were hurting. Then he heard a donkey coming down the road. Clipperty-clop, clipperty-clop.

'I wonder if this man will stop and help me,' thought Mr. Joab. 'I don't expect so. The people from his country aren't friends with the people from my country. He won't want to help *me*.'

But the man saw Mr. Joab.

'Poor man,' he thought, 'I must help him.'

He got off his donkey and gave Mr. Joab a drink of water. Then he put some ointment on his cuts, and bandaged them up. How surprised Mr. Joab was! Fancy this man helping him!

'You're too ill to walk,' said the man. 'You must ride on my donkey.'

So Mr. Joab got on to the donkey, and they began to move along. Quite often Mr. Joab nearly fell off because he was so ill, so the donkey had to go slowly. Clip-clop, clip-clop, went the donkey.

'Now we're almost there,' said the kind man. 'We'll stay at that house, and you'll soon be in bed.' They stopped outside the house, and the kind man lifted Mr. Joab off the donkey and carried him indoors. Then he put him on to a bed. 'You need a good rest,' he said, 'try to go to sleep.'

'Thank you,' said Mr. Joab. 'You're very kind.'

The next morning, the kind man said to the man whose house it was, 'Here are two silver coins. Mr. Joab can't pay you for staying here because his money was stolen. If you need any more money for him, I'll give it to you next

time I come.'

Soon Mr. Joab was better. How glad he was for the kind man who'd helped him!

A Prayer

Lord Jesus, thank You for all the people who are kind to me. Please help me to be kind to others. Amen.

A loving father

Two boys lived on a farm with their father. We don't really know what the names of the two boys were but we'll call them David and Daniel.

Sometimes Father said, 'I'm going to move the cows into another field today. Would you like to help me?' Sometimes Father said, 'I'm going to plant some seeds today. Would you like to help me?' David and Daniel liked to help Father. He was a good father and loved them very much.

When David and Daniel grew up, they still helped Father on the farm. Father had shown them how to do so many jobs. Now they could work by themselves. Father liked to see David and Daniel working on the farm.

'When I'm an old, old man,' thought Father, 'I shall give all my things to David and Daniel. I shall give some of my animals to David and some to Daniel. I shall give some of my money to David and some to Daniel. I want them to have everything that is mine.' He was a good father.

But Daniel didn't want to wait until Father was an old, old man. He wanted some of his things now. Daniel said to Father, 'I don't want to wait until you're old. Will you give me my money now, so that I can spend it?' Father

73

fetched his money, and gave some of it to David and some to Daniel. 'There you are,' he said.

Daniel didn't want to stay with his father. He didn't want to work on the farm any more. Daniel wanted to go away by himself and do just what he liked. So he did. Off he went, all alone, with the money Father had given him, which he kept in a little bag.

Daniel walked a long way, and he came to a busy town. There were lots of people. He'd never seen so many people anywhere near Father's farm. It was great fun! He didn't have to do any work here! He could do just what he liked. He had all the money Father had given him and he could spend it on all the things he wanted. One day he thought, 'I shall buy myself some very special clothes.' So he did. And he took some of the money that his father had given him out of the bag to pay for the clothes. Another day he thought, 'I shall have a very big party.' 'Come to my party,' he said to lots of people he met. So he bought plenty of things to eat and drink.

Every day he spent more of his money. 'I'm having a wonderful time,' he said. Daniel was so busy he'd forgotten about someone who was thinking about him. You haven't forgotten

74

about Daniel's father, have you? He was still at home. He wanted Daniel to come home again because he loved him so much.

One day, Daniel looked in his bag. 'Oh dear!' he thought. 'There are only two coins left.' He spent one of the coins. Then he had only one left. The next day he took out the last coin. 'I shall have to buy something to eat today with this coin,' he said. When he had spent that one he had no more money to buy anything else to eat. None of his friends wanted to give him anything. He was alone and very sad.

Can you remember who was at home loving Daniel and waiting for him to come back? Yes, it was his father. Every day, Father wondered, 'I wonder if Daniel will come home today?' Then he would look along the road. Every day he said, 'No, he's not coming today.'

But one day he looked out from his house and someone was coming along. He looked again. 'It's Daniel,' he said. 'He's coming home.' Father ran off quickly to meet him. He threw his arms round Daniel.

'Father, I'm sorry I was so unkind. I'm sorry I've been silly,' said Daniel.

'Come on indoors,' said Father. 'This is

wonderful. My son has come home again.'
He was a good father.

A Prayer

Dear Father God, I'm sorry I sometimes do naughty things which make You sad. Thank You for loving me all the same. Amen.

Jesus visits a family

Peter, Mrs. Peter, Grandmother and Andrew lived near the seaside. They lived in a little white house with a flat roof and stairs outside.

Mrs. Peter and Grandmother liked the house to be clean. Mrs. Peter swept the floor with the brush, 'sweep, sweep,' and then it was clean again. They needed water for cooking and drinking but there was no tap in their house. Mrs. Peter took a large water jar, put it on her head, and walked to the well to fetch the water. Then she carried it all the way home again, still on her head. Clever Mrs. Peter!

Grandmother stayed at home. She liked to be busy and she liked to look after Peter, Andrew and Mrs. Peter. She liked to do the cooking and make nice things for everyone to eat. Round and round went the flour in the bowl, as she began to make little rolls for supper. Gurgle, gurgle went the water as she mixed it with the flour. Pat, pat went her hands as she made the little round shapes. Grandmother liked doing the cooking.

When Peter and Andrew came home they

were so tired and hungry. Grandmother gave them some of her rolls and some fish she had cooked.

'Oh, Grandmother,' said Peter, 'this is a lovely supper. We're glad that you look after us.'

Quite often, Jesus came home with Peter and Andrew. He liked to be in their house. Those were very special days. Everybody liked it when Jesus came to dinner.

Grandmother was specially busy on those days, and she wanted the dinner to be the very best it could be. She would be hustling and bustling all the morning.

One day Grandmother wasn't well enough to get up. 'My head aches,' she said. 'I feel so hot all over. May I have a drink of water?' Mrs. Peter gave her some water to drink. Grandmother had to stay in bed. Mrs. Peter felt her head and her hands. 'You're very hot and ill,' she said.

Presently, Grandmother asked, 'Could you fetch me another drink of water?' Poor Grandmother! She couldn't get up to do any work. She just wanted drinks of water. Mrs. Peter, Peter and Andrew felt unhappy. Everybody loved Grandmother and now she was very ill.

Peter and Andrew were going to the church. 'Goodbye, Grandmother,' they said. 'Hurry up and get better. We'll see you when we come back.' And off they went looking sad. There were lots of other people in the church, and Jesus was there too.

When they came outside again, Jesus started

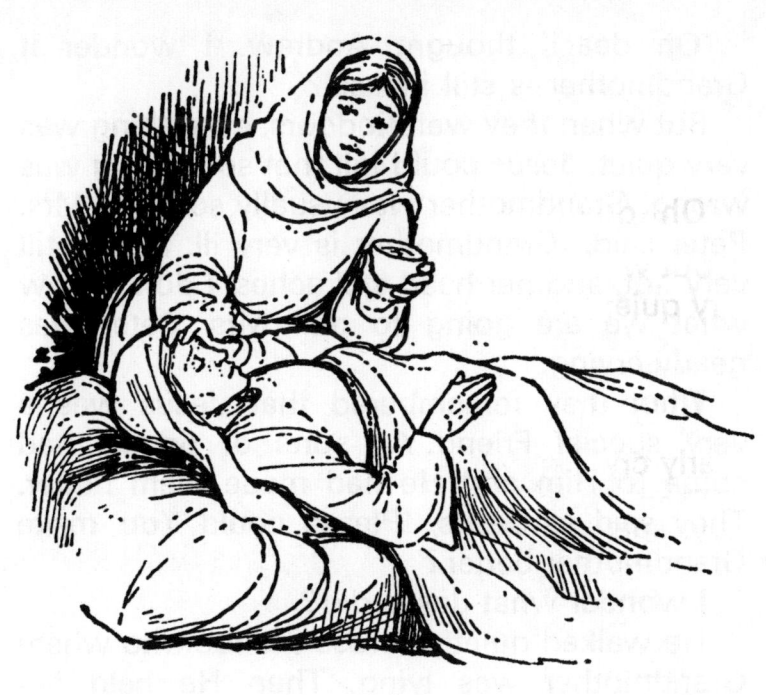

to walk home with Peter and Andrew. He was coming home to dinner. 'Oh dear!' thought Peter. 'I wonder if Grandmother is better? I wonder if she's been able to cook the dinner?'

'Oh dear!' thought Andrew. 'I wonder if Grandmother is still in bed?'

But when they went indoors, everything was very quiet. Jesus could tell that something was wrong. Grandmother was usually so busy. Mrs. Peter said, 'Grandmother is very ill. She's still very hot, and her head still aches. I don't know what we are going to do.' Mrs. Peter was nearly crying.

Then they remembered that Jesus was a very special Friend. All sorts of people had come to Him and He had made them better. They said to Jesus, 'Please could You make Grandmother better?'

I wonder what Jesus did?

He walked quietly across the room to where Grandmother was lying. Then He held her hand. It was very hot but quickly it became cooler, and Grandmother's head stopped aching, and she felt well again!

She really was better! She got straight out of bed, and can you guess what she began to do? That's right. She got out her flour and the food they were going to have for dinner. It wasn't very long before Jesus, Peter, Mrs. Peter, Andrew and Grandmother were all eating a lovely dinner, cooked by Grandmother.

A Prayer

Lord Jesus, You made that home so happy when You went there. Please make our home happy, too. Amen.

The storm

One evening, just as the sun was going down, Jesus was feeling very tired. All day long He'd been talking to people and helping them and making them better. It had made Him very tired. But still all the people came round Him, and they didn't know how tired He was.

So, He went down to the beach and His friends went with Him. Do you remember the names of some of His friends? There were Andrew, Simon, James and John. They were the fishermen who wanted to help Jesus. Then there were eight more. They could see the beautiful blue water with some fishing boats tied up there, too.

Jesus said, 'Let's get into a boat and go on the lake. We need to have some rest, and it will be quiet over there.'

They climbed into the boat, sat down, and began to row. Jesus settled Himself down in the back of the boat and wrapped His cloak around Him to keep Himself warm. In and out went the oars, splash, splash, and up and down went the boat, as they gently moved along the water. The water made a noise as it touched the sides of the boat, swish, swish, and the oars went splish, splash as the friends rowed. It was just as if the water was rocking the little boat like a baby's cradle, up and down, up and down, and Jesus was so tired that He was soon asleep with His head on a cushion. The friends kept on rowing gently, so as not to wake Him. In and out went the oars, splish, splash, and up and down went the boat. Swish, swish, went the water as it touched the sides of the boat.

But there were big clouds in the sky and it was getting very dark. Everything was very quiet. Then the friends began to feel the wind on their faces, and it blew into their hair and their clothes. The waves began to get higher and higher, and water began to splash all over them. The wind blew harder and the waves went crash on the sides of the boat. The little boat was rocking backwards and forwards, in and out, up and down, from side to side, and the friends thought it would turn right over and sink. And Jesus was still fast asleep.

At last the friends couldn't let Him sleep any more. They pulled at Jesus' sleeve and shouted, 'Lord, save us!'

Jesus woke up at once and saw how frightened they all looked. 'Why are you so afraid?' He asked. The wind was blowing all round and still the boat was tossing up and down, but then Jesus did a wonderful thing. He stood up in the tossing boat, with the wind

blowing His cloak and the sea pouring over His feet, and called, 'Peace . . . be still!'

The wind stopped blowing, the water stopped pouring into the boat, everything was still, and Jesus' friends weren't afraid any more. They began rowing on to the other side of the lake.

They knew that when Jesus was with them they were safe.

A Prayer

Dear Lord Jesus, please help me not to be afraid, because I know that You are with me. Amen.